WASHINGTON, DC

By Jacki Lippman Drucker • Illustrated by Chris Krupinski

Peeking Duck
BOOKS
ARLINGTON VIRGINIA

To our Favorite Sights, Silly and Otherwise

Suzanne, Douglas, Arielle & Hannah–JLD

Matthew, Andy & Katie–CK

Emily & Rachel–OH

Danielle & Devin–GP

Published by Peeking Duck Books, a division of Lion Park Press, Inc.
Arlington, Virginia

First Edition 10 9 8 7 6 5 4 3 2 1

Silly Sights Washington, DC
Library of Congress Catalog Card Number: 95-74712
ISBN 0-9647857-0-6

Concept and Editorial Direction by Orin Heend

Design by Gail Peck • Peck Studios, Inc. • Silver Spring, MD

Special thanks to Mary Susan Philp and Amy Morgan Buckli

For information about other Peeking Duck® books or quantity discounts on purchases of *Silly Sights Washington, DC* for educational, fund raising or special promotional purposes, please contact:
Marketing Department, Peeking Duck Books • PO Box 207 • Arlington, VA 22210
703-892-6992 • 1-800-800-8148

Printed in Mexico

In Washington, DC...

...You can see quite a lot,
Some things that are silly and some that are not.

You even may find the sights in this book,
If you carefully check every cranny and nook.

It's a joke, it's a hoax, is that what you say?
Perhaps you're not looking in quite the right way.

First open your mind, then close your eyes tight,
You can make them appear any day any night.

You'll be astonished, astounded, amazed as can be,
At the silliest sights you ever did see!

Will you ever see

In Washington, DC…

…A mile high mop

Drinking green soda pop

Throwing rings at the Washington Monument's top?

W

ill you ever see

In Washington, DC...

...A polka- dot bear

With a bow in her hair

Hogging Abraham Lincoln's very big chair?

Will you ever see

In Washington, DC…

…A whistling mouse

In a frilly red blouse

Painting bright yellow stripes on the President's house?

Will you ever see

In Washington, DC...

...A wizard named Nate

With the moon on a plate

At the Smithsonian Castle to in-line skate?

CHRIS KRUPINSKI

Will you ever see

In Washington, DC...

...A grouchy old gnome

With a porcupine comb

Making faces on top of the Capitol dome?

CHRIS KRUPINSKI

Will you ever see

In Washington, DC...

...A Van Gogh-like bee

Painting pictures with glee

All over the National Gallery?

Will you ever see

In Washington, DC...

...A serpent who's cool

In a hat with a jewel

Splishing and splashing in the reflecting pool?

CHRIS KRUPINSKI

Will you ever see

In Washington, DC...

...A magic emir

On a flying reindeer

Pulling butterflies from Thomas Jefferson's ear?

Will you ever see

In Washington, DC…

…An old airplane race

With a duck flying ace

Inside the Museum of Air and Space?

CHRIS KRUPINSKI

Will you ever see

In Washington, DC…

…Show offy cranes

Sporting top hats and canes

Tippy tap dancing on the Metro trains?

Will you ever see

In Washington, DC...

...A panda in blue

Eating yummy bamboo

Hawking chocolate fondue at the National Zoo?

CHOCOLATE
FONDUE

CHRIS KRUPINSKI

Will you ever see

In Washington, DC…

…A stork and a swan

Dressed in purple chiffon

Figure skating on top of the Pentagon?

CHRIS KRUPINSKI

Will you ever see

In Washington, DC...

...Sixty two kangaroos

Wearing pink ballet shoes

At the Kennedy Center to play their kazoos?

CHRIS KRUPINSKI

Will you ever see

In Washington, DC...

...A martian named Clem

With three eyes on a stem

In Georgetown at noon at Wisconsin and M?

W

THE WASHINGTON MONUMENT was built between 1848 and 1885 in honor of George Washington, first president of the United States. The Civil War, financing and other problems halted construction of the 555-foot high marble obelisk for 22 years. Look up about 150 feet from the base where the marble changes color. That is where construction was interrupted.

THE LINCOLN MEMORIAL includes 56 steps, 36 columns, and a 19-foot tall statue of our 16th president by sculptor Daniel Chester French. In 1865, when Abraham Lincoln died at the age of 56, our country had 36 states. Lincoln's Gettysburg and Second Inaugural Addresses are carved into the marble walls.

THE WHITE HOUSE, originally called the President's House, has been both home and office to every president except George Washington. The British burned it down during the War of 1812, but by 1817, it was rebuilt. There are 132 rooms, 9 of which are private living quarters.

THE SMITHSONIAN "CASTLE" houses an Information Center for the Smithsonian Institution, which operates numerous museums both on and off the Mall. The Smithsonian was established from the $500,000 that Englishman James Smithson willed to the United States in 1846 to increase knowledge.

THE CAPITOL, second oldest public building in Washington, D.C. after The White House, is where the Senate and House of Representatives meet. In 1800, senators, congressmen and the justices of the Supreme Court all moved from Philadelphia into the Senate building, the only part of the Capitol completed at the time. In 1814, British troops burned the Capitol. In 1863, the building as we see it today was finally completed.

THE NATIONAL GALLERY of Art exhibits in two buildings a wide variety of works ranging from DaVinci and Van Gogh to Rothko and Miro. In the East Building, which is itself a work of art, there is a giant mobile by Alexander Calder.

THE REFLECTING POOL, located between the Washington Monument and the Lincoln Memorial, is almost 2000 feet long. In it, you can see the reflections of both of these famous landmarks.

THE JEFFERSON MEMORIAL is dedicated to Thomas Jefferson, architect, inventor, author of the Declaration of Independence, and third president of the United States. The bronze sculpture of Jefferson, 19-feet tall, looks out over the Tidal Basin, which is surrounded by the city's famous cherry trees, a gift from Japan.

THE NATIONAL AIR & SPACE MUSEUM, the most popular museum in the world, chronicles the history of aviation. There you can see historic aircraft such as the Wright brothers' plane and the Apollo 11 command module, a moon rock and movies on a screen five stories high.

METRORAIL trains transport passengers around the Washington, D.C. metropolitan area on a system of tracks 81.5 miles long. Metro's deepest station, Forest Glen in suburban Maryland, is 21 stories (196 feet) underground.

THE NATIONAL ZOO or, more formally, the National Zoological Park, is a natural oasis in the heart of the city. It is home to lions, tigers and bears, and countless other animals from around the world, including Hsing-Hsing, a giant panda from China.

THE PENTAGON, a unique five sided building, our country's military headquarters, and the world's largest office building, is actually located across the Potomac River from Washington, D.C. in Arlington, Virginia. It contains 17.5 miles of hallways.

THE KENNEDY CENTER FOR THE PERFORMING ARTS showcases music, theater and dance from around the world in honor of John F. Kennedy, our 35th president. The red-carpeted Grand Foyer, which is longer than the Washington Monument is high, includes a 7-foot bronze bust of the former president and spectacular crystal chandeliers.

GEORGETOWN was established as a Maryland township in 1751. It did not become a part of Washington, D.C. until 1871. Once a wealthy tobacco port, its fortunes declined sharply when steamships and railroads took trade elsewhere. In the 1930's, young Washingtonians began restoring Georgetown's old buildings, turning it once again into a fashionable place to live.